You·Can·Draw
FANTASTIC
ANIMALS

A DK PUBLISHING BOOK

Project Editor Helen Drew
Art Editor Peter Radcliffe
Managing Editor Jane Yorke
Managing Art Editor Chris Scollen
US Editor Camela Decaire
Production Josie Alabaster

First American Edition, 1997
2 4 6 8 10 9 7 5 3 1
Published in the United States by DK Publishing, Inc.
95 Madison Avenue, New York, New York 10016

Visit us on the World Wide Web at
http://www.dk.com

Published in Great Britain by Dorling Kindersley Ltd.

A catalog record for this book is
available from the Library of Congress.

ISBN 0-7894-3889-5

Color reproduction by GRB, Italy
Printed in Belgium by Proost

Photography by Peter Anderson, Jane Burton, Andy
Crawford/Kit Houghton, Geoff Danin, Dave King, Bob
Langrish, Cyril Laubscher, Tracy Morgan, Steve Shott,
Kim Taylor, Barrie Watts, and Jerry Young.

DK would like to thank
Sarah Johnston for editorial assistance, Almudena Díaz
for DTP design, Mark Haygarth for jacket design, and
Sally Hamilton for picture research.

You·Can·Draw
FANTASTIC
ANIMALS

Grahame Corbett

Contents

DK

DK PUBLISHING, INC.

This book shows you how to quickly improve your animal drawings by following a few simple rules. First look at the proportions of the animal, then draw the basic outline shapes. Finally, sketch in guidelines to help you position the animal's features. The more you practice, the more realistic your drawings will be. Each page teaches you more about drawing the features of individual animals.

Looking at proportion

Before you start, study each animal carefully. Look at its position and at parts of the body that are aligned or similar in size. Use the measurements of the head to help you draw the animal in proportion.

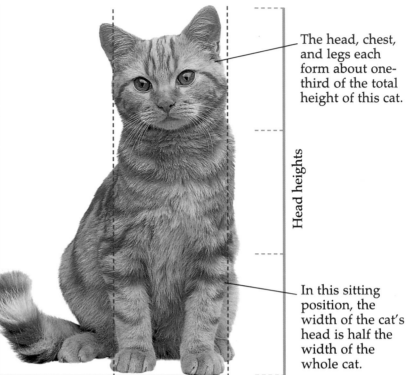

The head, chest, and legs each form about one-third of the total height of this cat.

Head heights

In this sitting position, the width of the cat's head is half the width of the whole cat.

Head widths

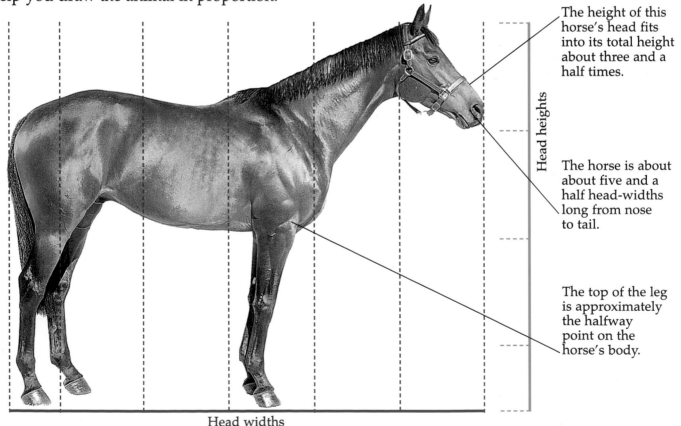

The height of this horse's head fits into its total height about three and a half times.

Head heights

The horse is about about five and a half head-widths long from nose to tail.

The top of the leg is approximately the halfway point on the horse's body.

Head widths

Using guidelines

The outline of an animal is easier to draw if you divide it into a few basic shapes in your imagination first. Draw these shapes on paper, making sure the proportions are correct.

Outline shapes

First divide the animal into simple shapes.

Basic outline shapes have been printed on animal photographs to help you.

Internal shapes

Next look for internal shapes that will help you draw a more detailed outline.

Outline shapes are drawn in blue to help you see them.

Draw lines to show the angles and lengths of legs, arms, and tails.

Blue guidelines show you how to position the ear.

Internal head shape

Eye sits on extension of snout line.

Guidelines

Finally, look for guidelines and shapes that will help you place facial features. Extensions of mouth, nose, and neck lines are often very useful.

Adding detail to your drawings

Experiment with colors and soft and hard pencils to color and shade in the details of the animal you are drawing.

Shade in dark areas of color first.

Use light cross-hatching for shadowy areas.

Use loose shading with longer strokes for long fur.

Draw light hairs and whiskers last, using a white pencil.

Use soft shading in a pale tone for the base color, then add detail on top.

Use a sharp pencil to add details, such as the long hairs of the mane.

Use loose shading for the texture and patterns of short fur.

Shading

Try using these techniques to finish off your drawings.

Loose shading uses lots of tiny, curved lines to show short fur and skin textures.

Cross-hatching can be used to show shadows. The more crossed lines you draw, the deeper the shadow effect.

Soft shading uses long, heavy pencil strokes that ease off to light strokes. Smudge with a finger for a soft effect.

Here you can try drawing the front view of a sitting cat. If you look at the proportions of its body in this position, you will notice that the head (from ear to chin) measures about one-third of the cat's total height. The body (from shoulder to shoulder) is about one-half of the width of the whole cat. Find out more about drawing cats' heads and fur opposite.

Look at the cat you wish to draw and see if its position makes any simple shapes that you can use to start your drawing.

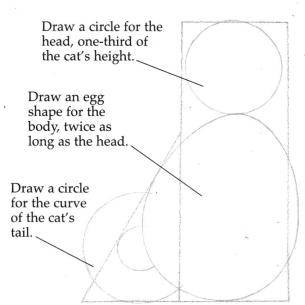

Sitting pretty

This sitting cat forms two basic outline shapes: a triangle and a tall rectangle. Use these to help you draw the cat's body shape.

Draw a circle for the head, one-third of the cat's height.

Draw an egg shape for the body, twice as long as the head.

Draw a circle for the curve of the cat's tail.

1 First draw the basic outline shapes as a guideline. Then start adding internal shapes for the head, body, and tail.

Draw in two triangles for the ears.

The nose and mouth form an oval shape.

Lightly draw in the legs, feet, and tail.

Draw in the main features of the cat's face. (See opposite page.)

Add detail to the body outline, legs, and feet.

Erase the guidelines you don't need.

Shading in the shadowy areas makes your drawing look three-dimensional.

Find out about drawing the fur opposite.

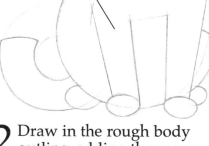

2 Draw in the rough body outline, adding the ear, neck, tail, leg, and foot shapes.

3 Improve the outline of the body. Start adding the facial features, as shown opposite.

4 Look for areas of light and shadow, and shade in the darker areas first.

Cat's head

These step-by-step instructions will help you draw a realistic cat's head every time.

Draw two crisscrossing guidelines from the center of the muzzle up to the ears.

The nose sits in the center of the muzzle.

The muzzle sits below the horizontal guideline.

1 Divide the cat's head circle into four. Add the ear and muzzle shapes.

The eyes sit on the horizontal line and are oval in shape. They are the width of the guidelines drawn up to the ears.

Draw two semicircles for the mouth.

2 Divide up the face with guidelines as shown, and outline the cat's features.

White highlights make the eyes look bright.

Soften the outline of the cat's face and ears with short, light pencil strokes.

3 Add detail to the face, eyes, and mouth. Take time to get the shapes right.

Soft fur

Use long pencil strokes to show areas with long fur and the curves of the cat's body.

Make short strokes with soft pencils for short fur.

4 To finish the face, draw in the texture and patterns of the fur. Start by shading in the darker areas.

Leave patches of white for the lightest areas.

Use a hard pencil for the spots on the cheeks.

Draw the long whiskers with a white pencil.

Portrait gallery

Here are some more cats for you to draw. Look at the proportions of each cat's head and see if you can draw the different types of fur.

Use soft pencils to reproduce the soft, fluffy fur.

This cat's markings are very distinctive.

This cat has very big ears on a small, triangular face.

Draw in pale whiskers with a white pencil.

Draw the long, fluffy fur with long pencil strokes.

This cat's ears and features are quite small in its face.

Manx cat

Snowshoe cat

Longhair cat

Dogs

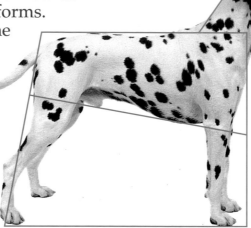

Before you start to draw a side view of a dog, look at the shapes it forms. The body and legs will form one shape, and the head another. Then look at the dog's proportions. Compare the height of the dog's head with the height of the whole dog, and compare the width of its head with the width of its body. Find out how to draw moving dogs opposite.

The head accounts for about one-fifth of the Dalmatian's height and a quarter of its whole width.

Standing dog
This dog forms two outline shapes. Its body and legs form a four-sided shape, and its head is an oval.

Study the angles of the legs before you sketch them in.

The body forms a sausage shape wider at one end.

1 Draw the basic shapes, add internal shapes for the body, and lines for the legs and tail.

The paws form circles at the ends of the legs.

Draw in guidelines to help you put in facial features. (See opposite page.)

Spotty coat
Make short, dark strokes with a hard black pencil to draw in the Dalmatian's spotted coat.

2 Draw in the rough outline of the body, sketching in the shape of the legs and tail.

Erase the guidelines you don't need.

Draw in a more rounded body outline.

Add the ear shape and eye position.

Sketch in the shapes of the legs and feet.

3 Improve the outline of your drawing. Add detail to the dog's head, as shown opposite.

Shade in the shadowy areas on the underside of the dog.

See how to finish the dog's head opposite.

4 Clean up your drawing. Shade the darker areas first, then add the details of the fur.

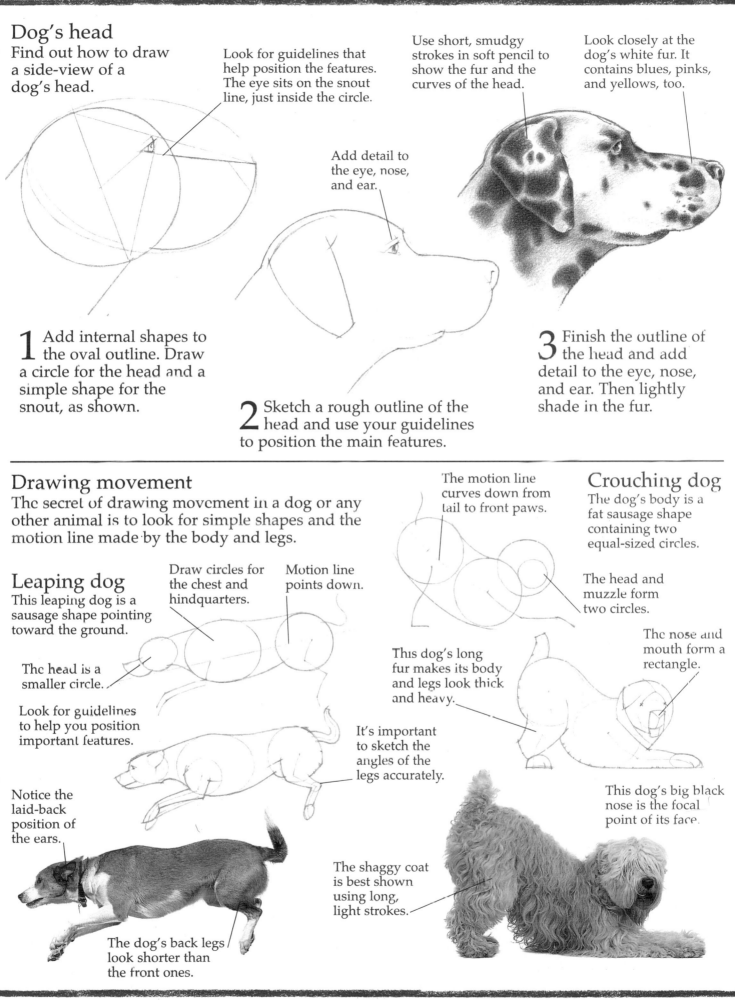

Dog's head
Find out how to draw a side-view of a dog's head.

Look for guidelines that help position the features. The eye sits on the snout line, just inside the circle.

Use short, smudgy strokes in soft pencil to show the fur and the curves of the head.

Look closely at the dog's white fur. It contains blues, pinks, and yellows, too.

Add detail to the eye, nose, and ear.

1 Add internal shapes to the oval outline. Draw a circle for the head and a simple shape for the snout, as shown.

2 Sketch a rough outline of the head and use your guidelines to position the main features.

3 Finish the outline of the head and add detail to the eye, nose, and ear. Then lightly shade in the fur.

Drawing movement
The secret of drawing movement in a dog or any other animal is to look for simple shapes and the motion line made by the body and legs.

Leaping dog
This leaping dog is a sausage shape pointing toward the ground.

The head is a smaller circle.

Look for guidelines to help you position important features.

Notice the laid-back position of the ears.

Draw circles for the chest and hindquarters.

Motion line points down.

The dog's back legs look shorter than the front ones.

It's important to sketch the angles of the legs accurately.

The motion line curves down from tail to front paws.

Crouching dog
The dog's body is a fat sausage shape containing two equal-sized circles.

The head and muzzle form two circles.

The nose and mouth form a rectangle.

This dog's long fur makes its body and legs look thick and heavy.

This dog's big black nose is the focal point of its face.

The shaggy coat is best shown using long, light strokes.

Horses and ponies

Here you can find out how to draw horses from the side. Look at the proportions of this horse – it has long legs, a powerful body, and a relatively small head. Its shiny coat shows the muscles underneath.

The head and neck form about one-third of the horse's total width.

The mid-height point of the horse is approximately the top of its front leg.

Horse body shapes

First draw the basic outline shapes of this standing horse. The body and legs form a large rectangle.

Draw two large circles for the chest and hindquarters.

The head is made of two circles joined together.

Sketch in lines for the legs and tail.

Notice how the angle of each part of the leg changes at each joint.

1 Draw internal shapes for the horse's head and body, and lines for the positions of the legs and tail.

Look out for points where the legs join the circles.

Lightly draw in the mane.

The nostrils and mouth sit in the small circle.

Erase the guidelines you don't need.

Study the shapes and angles of the legs, then lightly sketch them in.

2 Sketch in the rough body outline, adding head details and the shape of the legs and tail.

Fill in the mane using long strokes of your pencil.

See how to draw the head opposite.

Shade in lines of muscle on the legs and body.

3 Use smooth, smudgy strokes to shade in the darker areas of the coat. Use light colors for shiny areas.

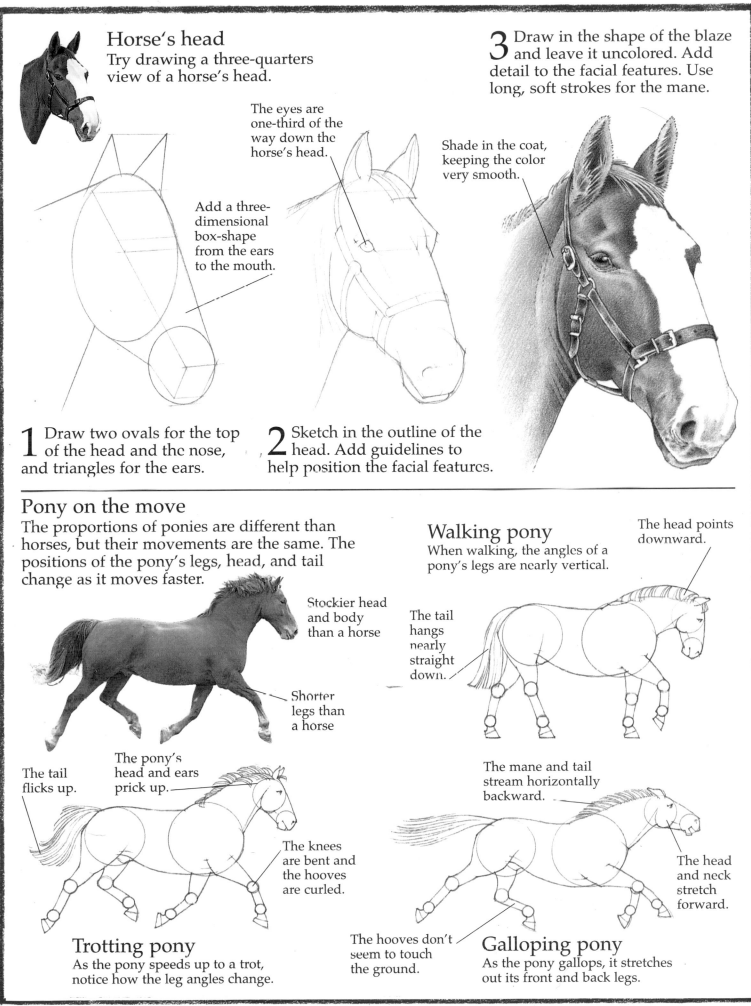

Horse's head

Try drawing a three-quarters view of a horse's head.

3 Draw in the shape of the blaze and leave it uncolored. Add detail to the facial features. Use long, soft strokes for the mane.

The eyes are one-third of the way down the horse's head.

Add a three-dimensional box-shape from the ears to the mouth.

Shade in the coat, keeping the color very smooth.

1 Draw two ovals for the top of the head and the nose, and triangles for the ears.

2 Sketch in the outline of the head. Add guidelines to help position the facial features.

Pony on the move

The proportions of ponies are different than horses, but their movements are the same. The positions of the pony's legs, head, and tail change as it moves faster.

Stockier head and body than a horse

Shorter legs than a horse

Walking pony

When walking, the angles of a pony's legs are nearly vertical.

The head points downward.

The tail hangs nearly straight down.

The tail flicks up.

The pony's head and ears prick up.

The knees are bent and the hooves are curled.

The mane and tail stream horizontally backward.

The head and neck stretch forward.

Trotting pony

As the pony speeds up to a trot, notice how the leg angles change.

The hooves don't seem to touch the ground.

Galloping pony

As the pony gallops, it stretches out its front and back legs.

Birds

Birds come in many shapes and sizes, from the tiniest hummingbirds to the tallest ostrich. Most birds have a rounded, streamlined shape. Here you can find out how to draw a small, perching bird. Opposite you can practice drawing birds' heads. Turn the page to find birds in flight.

Bird shapes
This bird forms two triangles. Its head is a quarter of its length.

1 Draw the basic outline shapes and add rounded internal shapes for the head and body.

Sketch in lines for the legs and feet.

Look for guidelines to help you position the eye, beak, and other facial features.

Sketch in curved shapes for the face, wing, and stomach.

Look for guidelines and shapes on the wing and tail feathers.

Add detail to the face and beak.

Erase the guidelines you don't need.

Improve the shape of the legs and feet.

2 Sketch in the outline of the bird, adding the beak, leg, and tail shapes.

Let the paper show through on light areas.

See how to color in feathers opposite.

Leave a white spot on the eye to make it glint.

3 Start adding detail to the bird's feathers. Use curved lines to show the roundness of the bird's body.

Color dark feathers first, leaving areas blank for the lighter feathers.

Shade pale, fluffy feathers with soft colors.

4 Color in areas of shadow first. Start at the head and work down to the tail. Draw in the leathery skin of the legs.

Feathers
Look for the lines, patterns, and shapes that different feathers form on the bird's body.

Tail feather

Chest feather

Front view of an owl's head

Try drawing this front view of an owl's head, then turn the page to draw it in flight.

Large eyes lie on the horizontal center line.

Sketch in the center line.

1 Draw two circles for the face. Add triangular guidelines for the eyes, forehead, and beak.

A heart-shaped ridge of feathers frames the face.

Look for guidelines to shape the eyes.

2 Sketch in the outline of the head and neck. Add details to the eyes and beak.

3 Lightly sketch in details of feathers around the face. Shade in areas of shadow to show the curves of the face.

Use areas of loose shading and dots of dark colors to show the feather patterns.

Side view of a parrot's head

Follow this step-by-step guide to drawing a parrot's head from the side.

Use guidelines from the beak to position the eye.

1 Draw an oval for the head. Add internal shapes for the eye, cheek, and beak.

Study the beak shapes carefully.

Add detail to the eye.

2 Sketch in the outline of the head and beak. Add pale outlines of facial features.

3 Shade in the darker areas on the beak. Let the paper show through in light areas.

Graduate your shading to show the contours of the beak and cheek.

Looking at heads

Try drawing these birds' heads. Their beak shapes and feather patterns are all very different.

The toucan has a huge, colorful beak.

Draw the simple shapes of the beak, face, and neck.

The short beak and stiff crest of feathers on this waxwing gives the head a square shape.

The imperial eagle has piercing eyes and a sharp, hooked beak!

The feathers seem to flow down the neck.

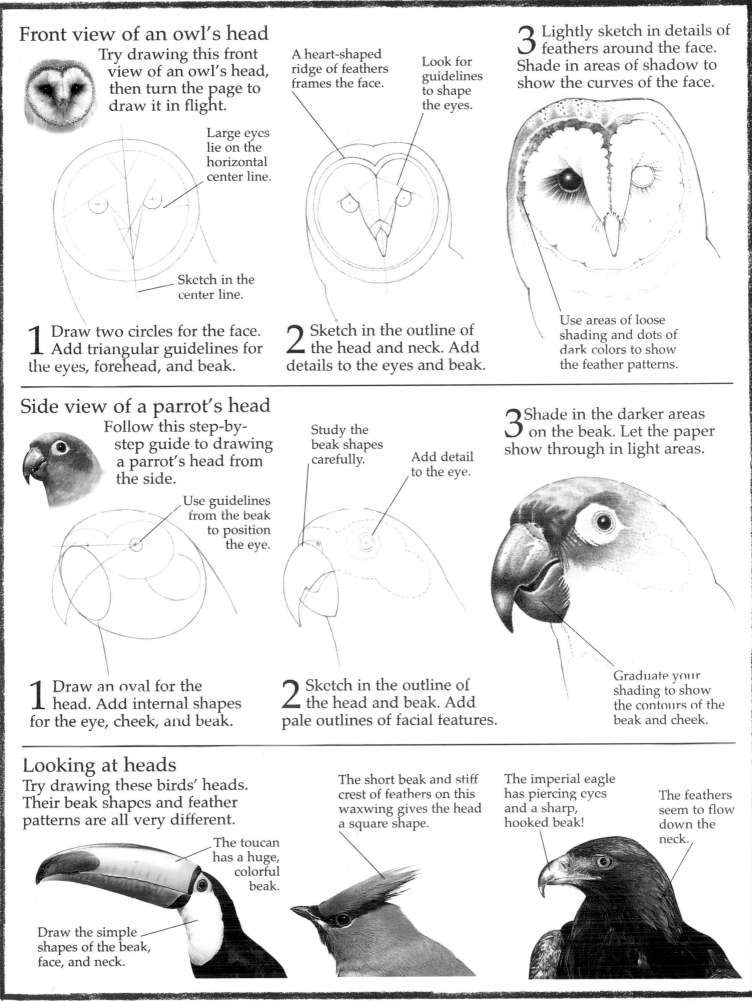

Flying birds

I t's difficult to draw a bird in flight, because it moves so quickly. However, you can practice drawing birds in different flying positions from pictures instead. Try sketching this owl first. Compare the length of the wings to the height of the owl.

Owl in flight
The outline shapes made by the wings and body of this owl are triangles.

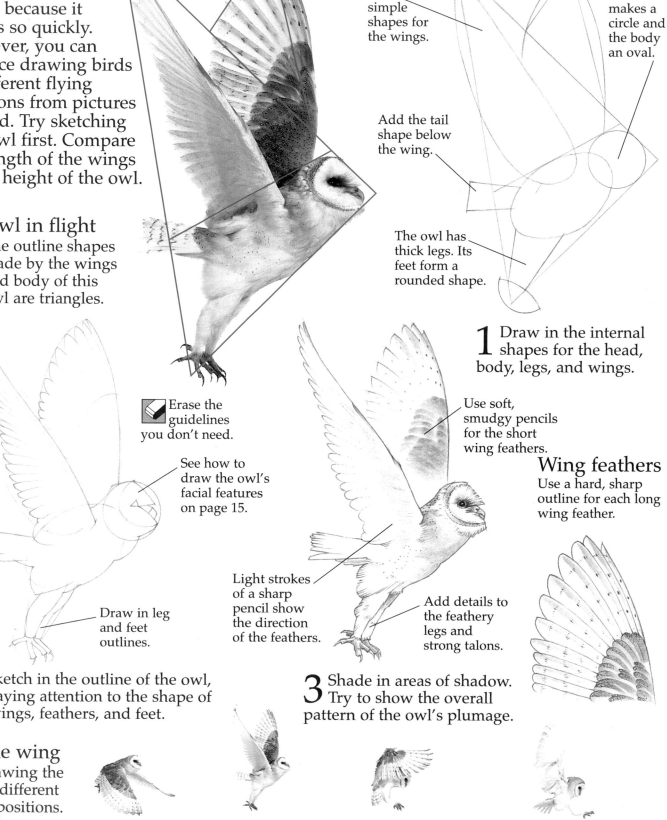

Add simple shapes for the wings.

The head makes a circle and the body an oval.

Add the tail shape below the wing.

The owl has thick legs. Its feet form a rounded shape.

1 Draw in the internal shapes for the head, body, legs, and wings.

Erase the guidelines you don't need.

See how to draw the owl's facial features on page 15.

Use soft, smudgy pencils for the short wing feathers.

Wing feathers
Use a hard, sharp outline for each long wing feather.

Light strokes of a sharp pencil show the direction of the feathers.

Add details to the feathery legs and strong talons.

Draw in leg and feet outlines.

2 Sketch in the outline of the owl, paying attention to the shape of the wings, feathers, and feet.

3 Shade in areas of shadow. Try to show the overall pattern of the owl's plumage.

On the wing
Try drawing the owl in different flying positions.

Bird families

Duck and duckling

Ducks and ducklings are similar shapes.

The duck has a small head on a long neck.

Use the beak and neck guidelines to position the eye.

The body and wing form ovals.

Soft, short pencil strokes give the idea of feathers.

Shade in shadowy areas.

Sketch in some of the longer wing feathers.

Draw in details of the webbed feet.

The duckling seems to have no neck!

Look for guidelines to help you place the eye and beak.

Sketch in the shapes and angles of the legs and feet.

Fill in the outline in yellow, adding tiny strokes of brown and orange.

Show the fluffy feathers with soft pencil strokes.

Chick and rooster

This rooster and chick are very different shapes.

The body and head are round.

The head is a circle with a triangular beak.

The wing and thigh are ovals.

Use short, soft strokes for the chick's fluffy outline.

Use longer pencil strokes on the wing and leg feathers.

The chick's eye sits just above and behind its beak.

Add claw and skin details to the feet.

The rooster has a tiny head, a large body, and a dramatic tail.

Add shapes for the comb and wattle.

Use a strong line for the rooster's outline.

Long tail feathers curl downward.

The rooster forms four linking, rounded shapes.

The wing is a soft triangle.

Draw in the long, curving tail feathers.

Take time adding details to the head.

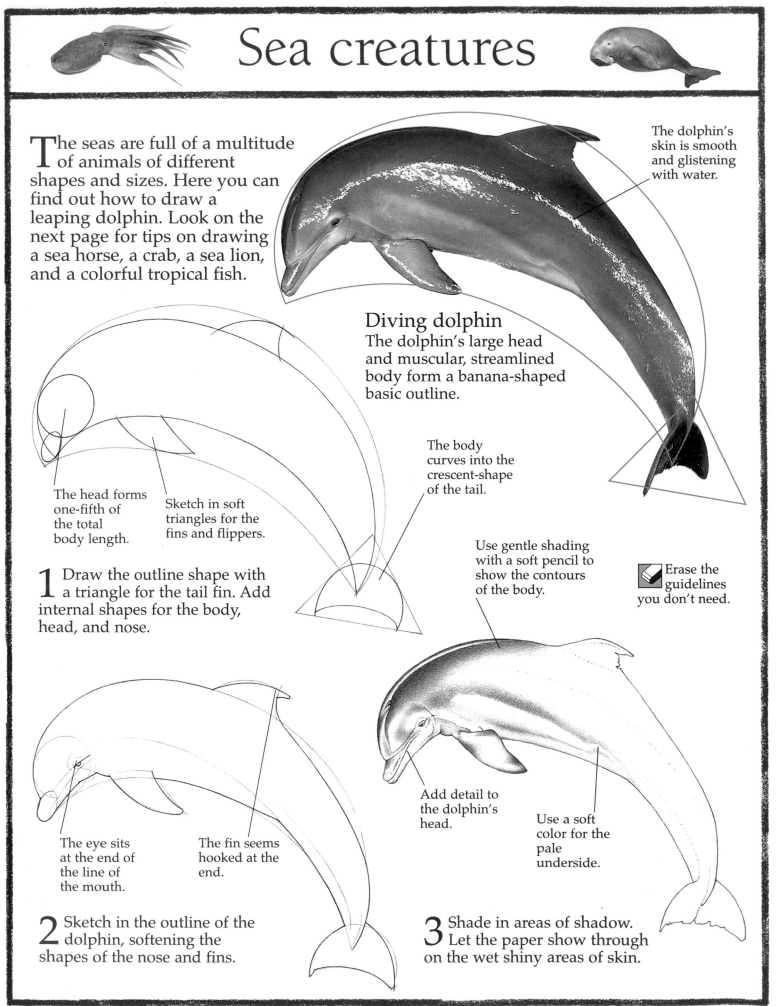

Sea creatures

The seas are full of a multitude of animals of different shapes and sizes. Here you can find out how to draw a leaping dolphin. Look on the next page for tips on drawing a sea horse, a crab, a sea lion, and a colorful tropical fish.

The dolphin's skin is smooth and glistening with water.

Diving dolphin
The dolphin's large head and muscular, streamlined body form a banana-shaped basic outline.

The body curves into the crescent-shape of the tail.

The head forms one-fifth of the total body length.

Sketch in soft triangles for the fins and flippers.

Use gentle shading with a soft pencil to show the contours of the body.

Erase the guidelines you don't need.

1 Draw the outline shape with a triangle for the tail fin. Add internal shapes for the body, head, and nose.

The eye sits at the end of the line of the mouth.

The fin seems hooked at the end.

Add detail to the dolphin's head.

Use a soft color for the pale underside.

2 Sketch in the outline of the dolphin, softening the shapes of the nose and fins.

3 Shade in areas of shadow. Let the paper show through on the wet shiny areas of skin.

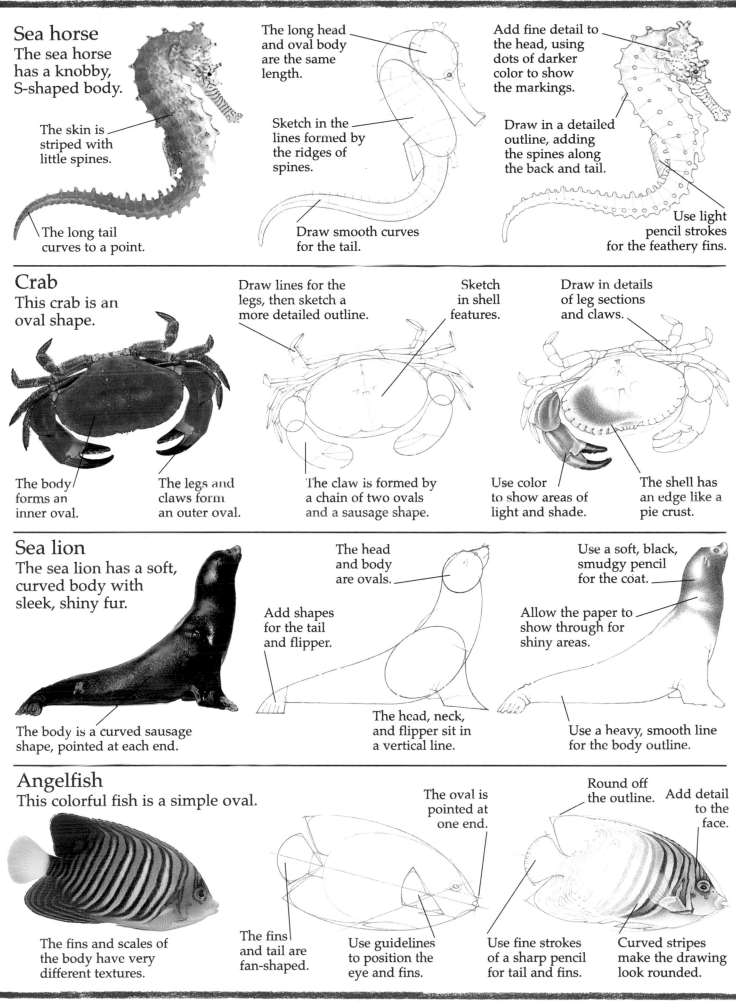

Sea horse

The sea horse has a knobby, S-shaped body.

The skin is striped with little spines.

The long tail curves to a point.

The long head and oval body are the same length.

Sketch in the lines formed by the ridges of spines.

Draw smooth curves for the tail.

Add fine detail to the head, using dots of darker color to show the markings.

Draw in a detailed outline, adding the spines along the back and tail.

Use light pencil strokes for the feathery fins.

Crab

This crab is an oval shape.

The body forms an inner oval.

The legs and claws form an outer oval.

Draw lines for the legs, then sketch a more detailed outline.

Sketch in shell features.

The claw is formed by a chain of two ovals and a sausage shape.

Draw in details of leg sections and claws.

Use color to show areas of light and shade.

The shell has an edge like a pie crust.

Sea lion

The sea lion has a soft, curved body with sleek, shiny fur.

The body is a curved sausage shape, pointed at each end.

The head and body are ovals.

Add shapes for the tail and flipper.

The head, neck, and flipper sit in a vertical line.

Use a soft, black, smudgy pencil for the coat.

Allow the paper to show through for shiny areas.

Use a heavy, smooth line for the body outline.

Angelfish

This colorful fish is a simple oval.

The fins and scales of the body have very different textures.

The fins and tail are fan-shaped.

Use guidelines to position the eye and fins.

The oval is pointed at one end.

Round off the outline.

Add detail to the face.

Use fine strokes of a sharp pencil for tail and fins.

Curved stripes make the drawing look rounded.

Here you can find out how to draw some of the world's most amazing animals. All have unusual proportions and special features, from a tall giraffe with its elegant neck, to a bounding kangaroo with its powerful back legs.

Note how the color of the giraffe's coat gradually pales on its legs.

The head forms a small triangle.

The neck and legs each form two-fifths of the giraffe's height.

Giraffe

The body and legs of the giraffe form a tall rectangle and the head a triangle. The body accounts for one-fifth of the giraffe's height.

The head and body shapes are joined together by two long, curved lines.

Draw a long oval for the giraffe's rounded body.

Sketch in long lines for the legs and tail.

1 Draw the outline shapes and add the internal shapes for the head, neck, and body.

The eye and ear lie on the line of the mouth.

Erase the guidelines you don't need.

Patterned fur

Shade the dark patches of the coat first, then fill in with pale, soft shading.

Draw ovals for the powerful muscles of the chest and hindquarters.

The joints of the knees and ankles are rounded.

Use long, soft pencil strokes for the tail.

Use a soft pencil to shade in the faded pattern on the legs.

Add detail to the head using a sharp pencil to make dots and fine lines.

Use short, sharp strokes of different weights for the mane.

Add detail to the legs, showing the joints and hooves.

2 Sketch a rough outline, adding shape to the head, legs, and hooves. Notice the points where the legs join the body.

3 Finish the outline of the giraffe. Use soft, feathery lines to show the lines of the muscles and any folds of skin.

Camel

This camel has a heavy body with two prominent humps and thin legs.

The heavy body forms two-thirds of the camel's length.

The hindquarters are thin.

The neck is low and curved with a thick, hairy mane.

The body is an oval with two flat-topped humps.

The eyes lie at the top of the oval on the lower line of the neck.

Draw a broken outline to show the hairy coat.

Use a sharp pencil to add details to the head and fur.

Kangaroo

The main features of this kangaroo are its upright position and powerful hindquarters.

The head is only one-sixth of the kangaroo's total height.

The kangaroo appears to be resting on its long tail.

Long, flat feet

The ears, head, chest, upper arms, lower body, and upper legs line up vertically.

The head, nose, chest, lower body, and thigh muscles are ovals.

Take time to draw in the shapes of the legs and feet.

Add circles for joints.

The eye sits midway between the nose and the ears.

Dense cross-hatching shows the thick fur.

Use a fine, broken line for the outline.

Use soft, dotted lines to show folds of skin.

Elephant

The elephant has a heavy body with thick legs and a long trunk. The skin is very wrinkly.

The legs and body are of equal height.

The head is one-third of the elephant's length.

The body is a large oval and the head is a circle.

The eye lies on the center line of the trunk.

The trunk is the same length as the legs.

Use close lines of dots to show folds in the wrinkly skin.

Use a smudgy, soft pencil to show the areas of light and shadow on the elephant's body.